To: _____

From: _____

INSPIRATIONAL QUOTES
FOR A
BEAUTIFUL DAY

50 Inspirational Picture Quotes to Brighten Your Day

DONNA MARTINS

Copyright © 2019 by Donna Martins
Cover and interior design © 2019 by Inspirational Grace LLC

All rights reserved. No part of this book may be reproduced, stored in a retrieval system or transmitted in any form or by any means, electronic, mechanical, photocopying, recording or otherwise, without written permission from its publisher, Inspirational Grace LLC.

Each quote herein is an original quote authored by Donna Martins.

Photo Credits
Front cover: Bess Hamiti/Pixabay
Back cover: Margriet Forsten/Pixabay
Photo collection: Pixabay

Published by Inspirational Grace LLC
P.O. Box 310, Park Forest, IL 60466
(312) 971-9980
info@inspirationalgrace.com

First Edition
ISBN: 978-1-7327357-0-5

Printed in the United States of America

Dedicated to all the underprivileged children that will benefit from the proceeds of this book.

Introduction

We live in a fast-paced society where millions of people wake up every morning heading off to work, parents getting children ready for school, grabbing coffee and breakfast on-the-go. Life can get so busy that we often forget to stop and breathe.

We are all going through different phases in life but our minds and souls need to be continuously rejuvenated. Whatever phase of life you are in at this moment, resolve to instill a daily dose of inspiration into your busy schedule, laugh often and surround yourself with positive people.

Inspirational Quotes for a Beautiful Day is an uplifting visual collection that will exude inspiration to enhance your day.

Encapsulated within this book are inspirational quotes written concisely with you in mind. I encourage you to take a break and flip through to find a quote that resonates with you and meditate on it throughout the day.

Take life one day at a time and seek to find beauty in everything.

Enjoy Reading and Be Inspired!

Donna Martins

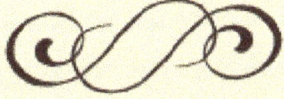

You woke up this morning. Smile!

IT'S A SIGN THAT YOU'RE GOING TO MAKE IT.

My circle can only accommodate the five people that will *advise, challenge, develop, empower & inspire* me.

Eliminate the complications of life and live simply.

Wake up each morning and gaze at the skies, the birds in the air and let the sun shine on you as a reminder that God still has a plan for your life.

Other things may come and go but books will always be in vogue. The wise invest in it.

Give a hug. Give a smile.

It's healing to the soul.

You're uniquely designed

TO BE
JUST YOU

nothing more...

INSIDE YOUR PASSION LIES YOUR PURPOSE

DISCOVER IT AND LIFE WILL BE SO MUCH FUN!

Today is as fresh as the morning flowers so I choose to make it just beautiful!

Yesterday is ancient history.

TODAY IS BRAND NEW AND A GREAT ONE TOO...

so be happy and enjoy every minute of it!

SHARE A SMILE WITH *a stranger*

Maximize today. It has great potential!

Laughter

REFRESHES THE SOUL AND ENHANCES YOUR YOUTH.

I owe it to myself to make today better than yesterday.

Be the person others can call for a good laugh!

Envision yourself

not as you are but as who you want to be.

Compete

WITH NO MAN BUT YOURSELF

At the end of each day, declutter your mind to make room for fresh dreams...

POSITIVITY
IS CONTAGIOUS!

Make a choice to surround yourself
with people that carry its traits.

WHEN LIFE GETS YOU DOWN,
SOAK YOUR MIND WITH SOME

Positive Affirmations!

BE A
VORACIOUS READER
IT'S
CRUCIAL TO
SELF-DEVELOPMENT

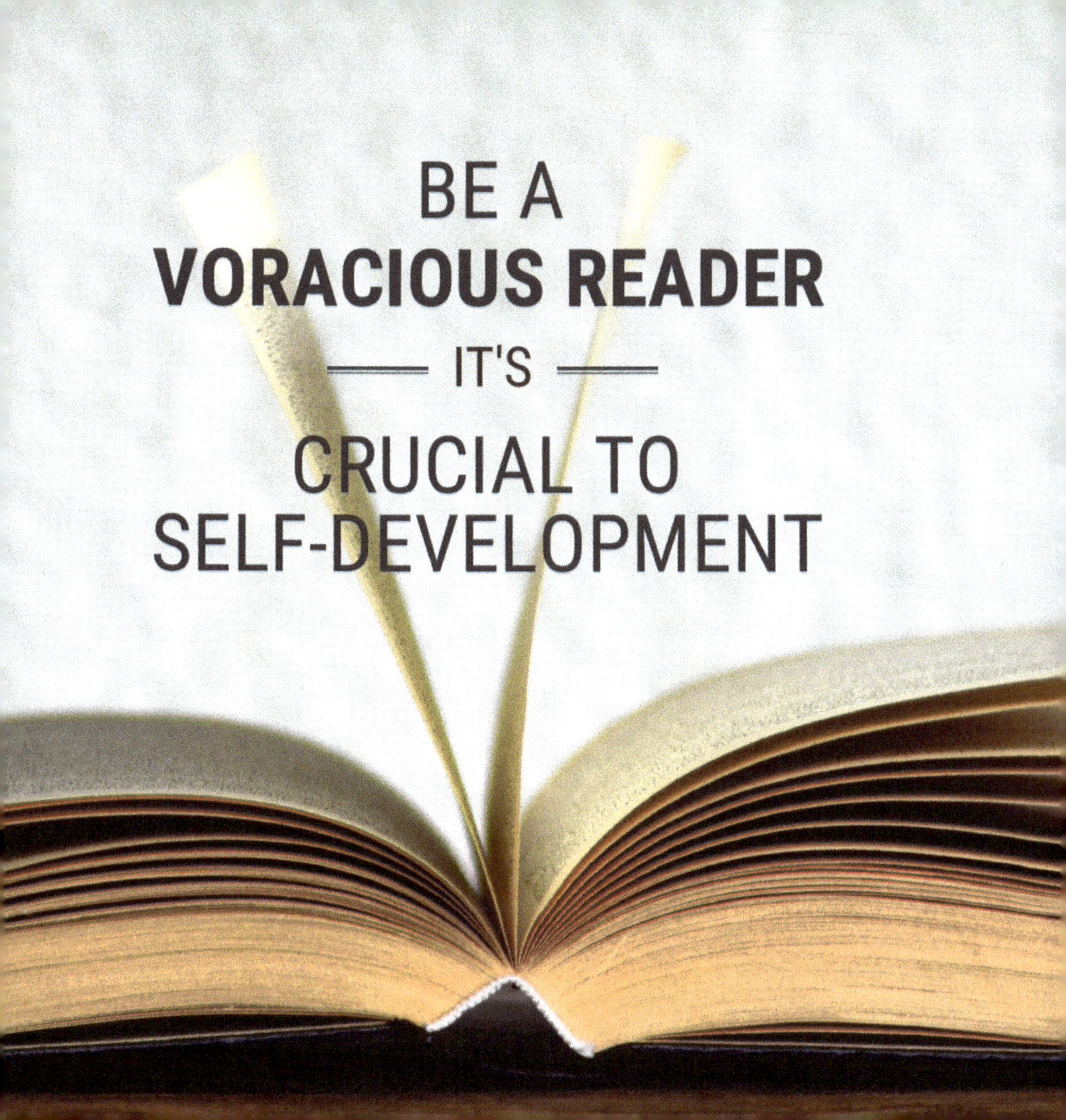

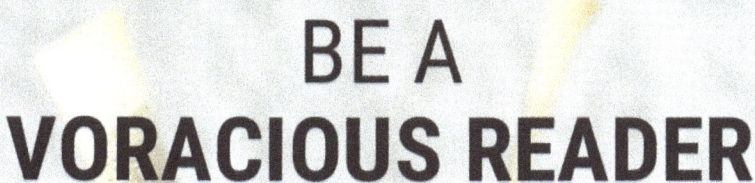

There are two points of direction in life – YESTERDAY & TODAY.

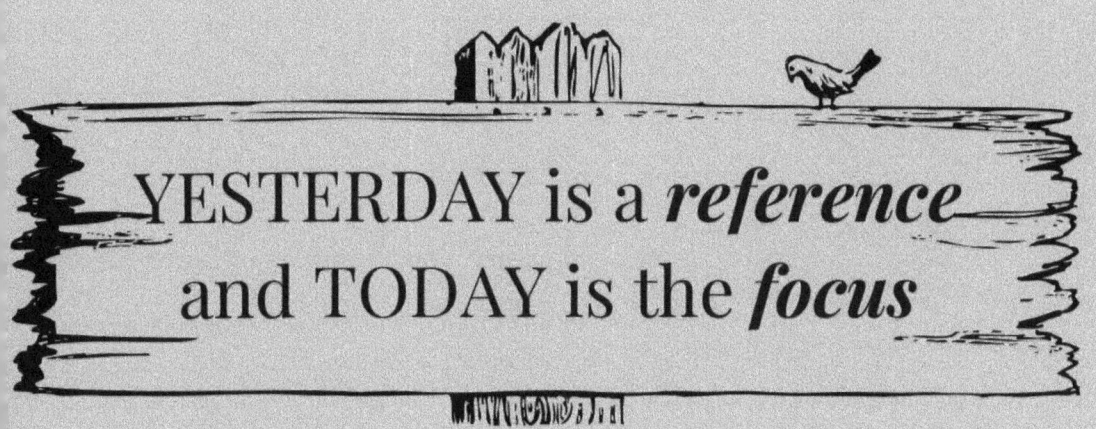

YESTERDAY is a *reference* and TODAY is the *focus*

YOU'RE NEVER TOO OLD OR TOO LATE TO FOLLOW YOUR DREAMS AS LONG AS YOU START NOW.

TAKE TIME OFTEN TO RELAX AND REJUVENATE.

Reward yourself for your hard work.

PROCRASTINATION
is the king of delays!

I'm convinced every day is a good day; that's why we use the greetings – good morning, good afternoon and good evening.

I HAVE THE POWER TO MAKE TODAY BETTER WITH MY WORDS AND ACTIONS SO I CHOOSE TO DO JUST THAT!

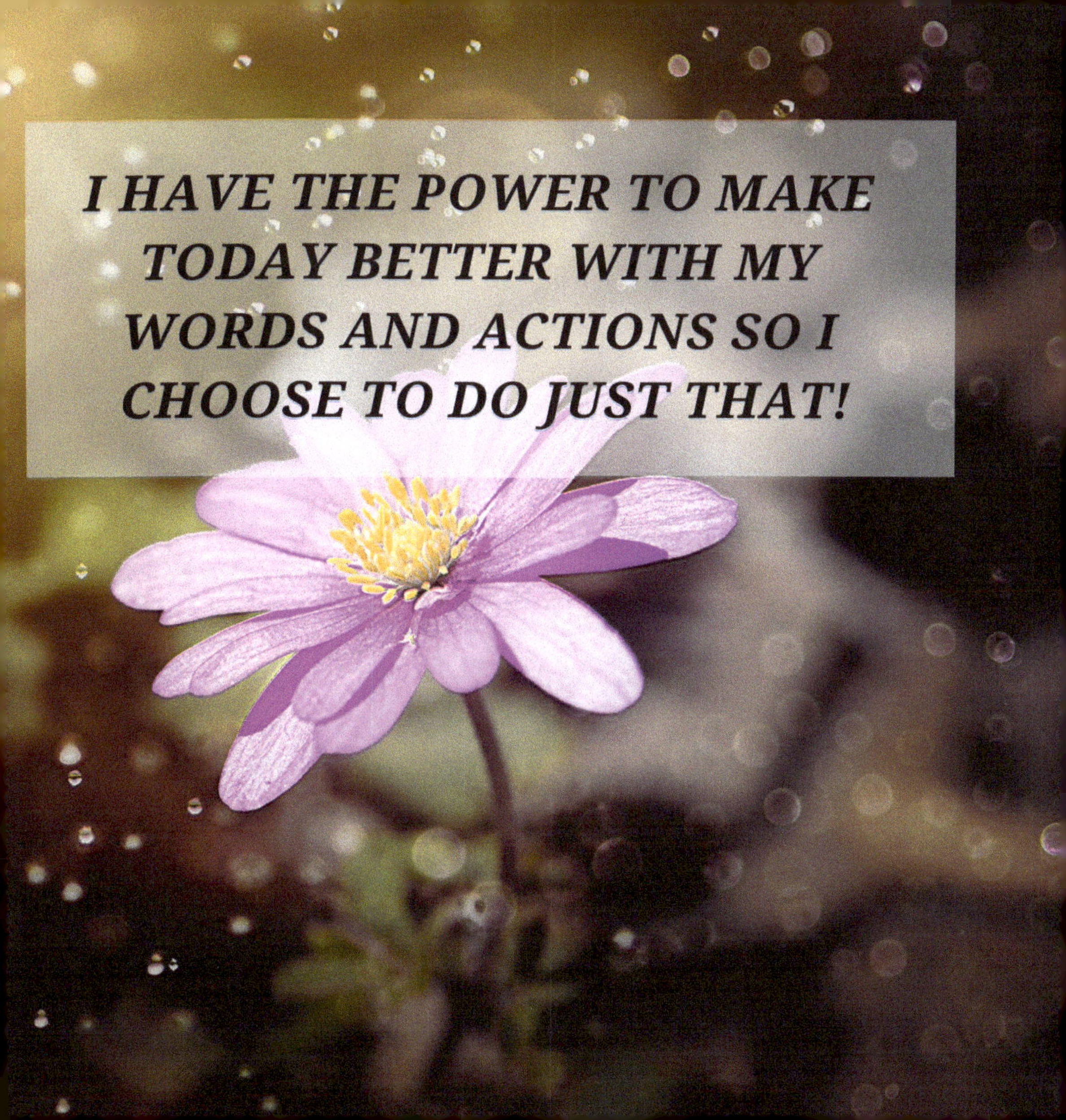

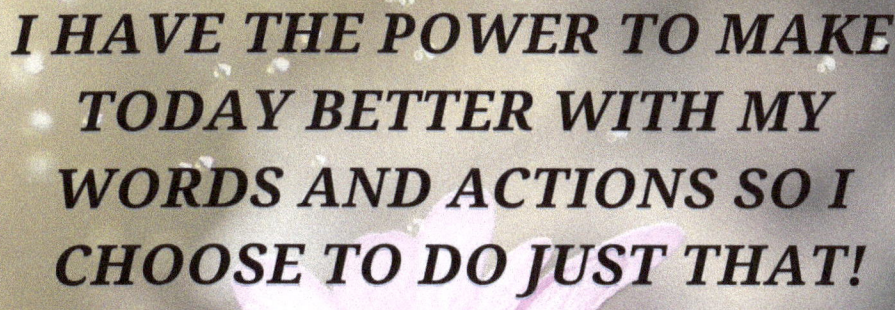

Everyone grows by learning. When you stop learning, you stop growing... so keep learning and growing!

LET TODAY BE THE DAWN OF

Fresh Possibilities!

COMMAND THE DAY AND PRIORITIZE IT WELL, OTHERWISE DISTRACTIONS WILL.

> Don't beat yourself up about yesterday's mistakes. Make up for it today.

Let the sunbeam shine through and all you'll ever see is a reflection of the bright side of life.

If you can inspire just one person,

you've made a difference!

365 Days = 1 Year of *Possibilities.* Start Living Today to Achieve *365 Possibilities* of a Greater *YOU!*

Dear Reader,

I hope that you have been inspired by reading this book. My wish is that you will hold on to the quotes that resonate with you, spread the inspiration and make someone else's day simply beautiful.

Thank you for being a part of my inspirational journey!

Donna

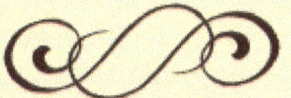

www.ingramcontent.com/pod-product-compliance
Lightning Source LLC
Chambersburg PA
CBHW061127070526
44584CB00033B/4247